# Financial Accounting

## Essentials You Always Wanted To Know

**VIBRANT**
PUBLISHERS

# Financial Accounting

## Essentials You Always Wanted To Know

Hardback ISBN-10: 1-949395-09-X
Hardback ISBN-13: 978-1-949395-09-9

Paperback ISBN-10: 1-946383-66-X
Paperback ISBN-13: 978-1-946383-66-2

Library of Congress Control Number: 2011927075

The publisher wishes to thank Kalpesh Ashar (India) for his valuable inputs to this edition

Vibrant Publishers books are available at special quantity discount for sales promotions, or for use in corporate training programs. For more information please write to **bulkorders@vibrantpublishers.com**

Please email feedback / corrections (technical, grammatical or spelling) to **spellerrors@vibrantpublishers.com**

To access the complete catalogue of Vibrant Publishers, visit **www.vibrantpublishers.com**

# Table of Contents

Dear Reader,

Thank you for purchasing **Financial Accounting Essentials You Always Wanted To Know.**
We are committed to publishing books that are content-rich, concise and approachable
enabling more readers to read and make the fullest use of them. We hope this book
provides you the most enriching learning experience.

This **Self-Learning Management Series** intends to give a jump start to working
professionals, whose job roles demand to have the knowledge imparted in a B-school but
haven't got a chance to visit one. This series is designed to address every aspect of
business from HR to Finance to Marketing to Operations, be it any industry. Each book
includes basic fundamentals, important concepts, standard and well-known principles as
well as practical ways of application of the subject matter. The distinctiveness of the
series lies in that all the relevant information is bundled in a compact form that is very
easy to interpret.

Should you have any questions or suggestions, feel free to email us at
**reachus@vibrantpublishers.com**

Thanks again for your purchase.

– Vibrant Publishers Team

# Books in
# Self-Learning Management Series

**Cost Accounting and Management**
**Essentials You Always**
**Wanted To Know**
ISBN: 978-1-946383-62-4

**Marketing Management**
**Essentials You Always**
**Wanted To Know**
ISBN: 978-1-949395-04-4

**Project Management**
**Essentials You Always**
**Wanted To Know**
ISBN: 978-1-946383-60-0

**Financial Management**
**Essentials You Always**
**Wanted To Know**
ISBN: 978-1-946383-64-8

**Principles of Management**
**Essentials You Always**
**Wanted To Know**
ISBN: 978-1-946383-93-8

**Business Strategy**
**Essentials You Always**
**Wanted To Know**
ISBN: 978-1-946383-98-3

**Financial Accounting**
**Essentials You Always**
**Wanted To Know**
Paperback ISBN: 978-1-946383-66-2
Hardback ISBN: 978-1-949395-09-9

For the most updated list of books visit
# www.vibrantpublishers.com

**facebook.com/vibrantpublishers**

# Chapter **1**

# Accounting Systems

An accounting system helps capture and organize information related to business transactions. Depending upon the focus it can be divided into two types:

  a)  Financial Accounting and

  b)  Managerial Accounting.

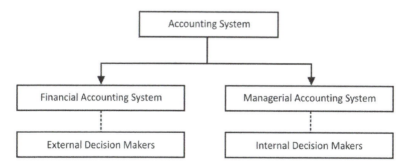

A Financial Accounting system contains financial statements and disclosures meant for decision makers external to the company. A Managerial Accounting system contains detailed plans and performance reports meant for decision makers within the company.

## Financial Accounting Systems

A financial accounting system is a system that serves the dual purpose of keeping track of transaction information and helping organize and evaluate this information primarily meant for external decision makers. The part related to keeping track of information is termed as "Bookkeeping", which is related to recording an activity, like taking a loan, paying a supplier, or receiving a payment. The other part related to organizing information for evaluation is termed as "Financial Statement", which consists of summarised information on the business activities that help evaluating the health of the business. Bookkeeping is done first and then the captured data is organized and evaluated as part of Analysis stage.

### Financial Accounting System

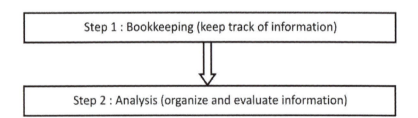

| Step 1 : Bookkeeping (keep track of information) |
| --- |

| Step 2 : Analysis (organize and evaluate information) |
| --- |

# Need for Financial Accounting Systems

Consider an example that some company buys equipment from another company and pays for it after 10 days. It also produces certain goods and sells 100 units to its customers and receives payment after 30 days. Assume that it also had to raise capital through a bank loan to buy the equipment and produce the goods. If none of these transactions were recorded anywhere then it would be impossible to know how much the company currently owes or needs to receive and hence the health of the company cannot be determined. Hence, bookkeeping (or recording of these transactions) is required by all companies.

Now assume that all transactions are recorded through a bookkeeping system and they are all presented to the external decision makers, like banker and investor. It would make it too difficult for them to wade through so many different transactions to figure out how the company was doing. Hence, financial statements are created from the recorded transactions so as to summarize all transactions in a few well-known heads of accounts to easily read the information and make decisions.

# Financial Statements

There are three main components to a company's financial statements:

a) Balance Sheet,

b) Income statement (even called Profit and Loss statement)

c) Statement of Cash Flows.

These days, financial statements also contain several mandatory and voluntary disclosures.

Below are simple examples of the three main components

## Balance Sheet

| Assets | | Liabilities | |
|---|---|---|---|
| Cash | $ 500.00 | Long-term loans | $ 8,000.00 |
| Land | $4,000.00 | Short-term liabilities | $ 2,000.00 |
| Equipment | $ 12,000.00 | | |
| Other assets | $ 3,500.00 | Equity | |
| | | Owner's investment | $ 10,000.00 |
| Total | $ 20,000.00 | Total | $ 20,000.00 |

A Balance Sheet shows a snapshot of how many resources (assets) a company owns, the company's obligations (liabilities) and the money invested by the owners (equity). As seen this is a summarized view that makes it easy to read as against reading each and every transaction of the company. It may also be noted that the total value of assets is exactly equal to the total value of liabilities and equity. It is always so and hence the name, Balance Sheet.

## Income Statement

| | | |
|---|---|---|
| Revenues | | $15,000 |
| **Expenses:** | | |
| Cost of raw materials | $5,000 | |
| Salaries | $2,500 | |
| Interest | $500 | |
| Income tax | $800 | |
| Other expenses | $1,000 | |
| Total expenses | | $9,800 |
| Net Income | | $5,200 |

An Income Statement (also known as Profit and Loss Statement) reports the revenue earned by the company over a period of time and the expenses incurred. This gives one of the most important measures of a company's health, called Net Income (also called Net Profit). If the expenses are more than revenue, then it results in a loss and the Net Income will be negative (shown in brackets as ($5,200)) as below.

| | | |
|---|---|---|
| Revenues | | $15,000 |
| **Expenses:** | | |
| Cost of raw materials | $10,000 | |
| Salaries | $5,000 | |
| Interest | $2,000 | |
| Income tax | $1,500 | |
| Other expenses | $1,700 | |
| Total expenses | | $20,200 |
| Net Income | | ($5,200) |

## Statement of Cash Flows

| | | |
|---|---|---|
| Cash from Operating activities: | | $5,000.00 |
| **Cash used for Investing activities:** | | |
| Purchase of property and equipment | ($3,500.00) | |
| Other investments | ($500.00) | |
| | | ($4,000.00) |
| **Cash from Financing activities:** | | |
| New bank loans | $1,500.00 | |
| Repayment of old loans | ($500.00) | |
| Payment of cash dividends | ($300.00) | |
| | | $700.00 |
| Net increase in cash during the year | | $1,700.00 |

The Statement of Cash Flows reports that amount of cash collected and paid by a company in the given period. Each cash transaction is divided into three types of activities – operating, investing, and financing. It shows the net increase (or net decrease) of cash with the company at the end of the period.

## Purpose of Financial Statements

External parties who need to make decisions about investing in a company, extending a loan to the company or even extending a credit period to the company, do so on the basis of financial statements. Below diagram shows how financial statements are used.

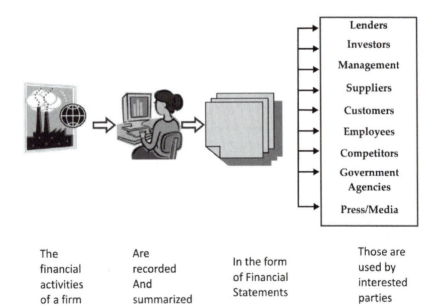

| The financial activities of a firm | Are recorded And summarized | In the form of Financial Statements | Those are used by interested parties |
|---|---|---|---|

Below are the main users of financial statements.

## Lenders

Lenders want to ensure that the company would be in a position to pay interest on a regular basis and the principle at maturity. These are generally banks, individuals, financial institutions and even other companies.

## Investors

Individual as well as corporate investors invest in a company if they feel that the company can provide attractive returns based on the risk profile of the company. They can ascertain this by looking at the company's financial statements and assume that the past performance is also representative of the future.

## Management

Although the management has a more detailed view by way of managerial accounting, there are still things in the financial statement that the management uses, like sales growth, profit margins, cash available etc.

## Suppliers

Extending supplier credit is a norm in most industries but suppliers are generally more comfortable extending greater credit periods or greater credit amounts to those companies who they feel would be in a better position to make the payment on the agreed date. They do so by looking at the company's financial statement that provides information about the financial strength and cash available with the company. They would also look at the company's past payment record to make a decision.

## Customers

There are some goods which require a good deal of after-sales support, like aeroplanes. Customers would want to know that the aeroplane manufacturer will not go out of business after they buy the plane from them. Financial statements help them gauge the company's financial strength.

## Employees

Financial statements often determine employees' bonus, pension, health care benefits etc. A financially strong company is also preferred by employees looking for a secure job.

## Competitors

Companies often look at the competitor's financial statements to compare their relative performance in terms of revenue, profit, margins etc. This information helps companies to benchmark the best in the industry and devise plans to match or better them.

## Government Agencies

Federal and state governments, IRS, SEC and other agencies frequently refer to the financial statements of companies to ensure investors' safety and to make policy decisions.

## Press/Media

Whenever the press wants to report about a company it can find a good amount of information in the company's financial statements. Significant events like large drop in profits, huge losses, and questionable practices are all generally based on the data present in the financial statements.

## Financial Accounting Standards

In the United States, *FASB* (Financial Accounting Standards Board) sets standards for financial accounting, including financial statements. The accounting rules are described as *GAAP* (Generally Accepted Accounting Principles).

Apart from *FASB*, there are other agencies that impact accounting standards and practice as below:

a) SEC (Securities and Exchange Commission) regulates US stock exchanges and seeks to create a fair information environment in which investors can buy and sell stocks without fear that companies are hiding or manipulating financial data.

b) AICPA (American Institute of Certified Public Accountants) is a professional organization of certified public accountants (CPAs) in the US. The CPAs provide business advice to companies related to accounting issues.

c) PCAOB (Public company Accounting Oversight Board) inspects the audit practices of registered audit firms.

d) IRS (Internal Revenue Service) establishes rules related to how income is to be taxed.

e) IASB (International Accounting Standards Board) develops common set of worldwide accounting standards.

# Solved Examples

**1.1 Why would the following individuals or groups be interested in a firm's financial statements?**

**a) Current shareholders of the firm**

**b) Creditors of the firm**

**c) Management of the firm**

**Solution:**

a) Current shareholders of the firm

The current shareholders of the firm would look at the financial statements for 3 reasons – to decide if the stock is worth holding or selling, whether additional investment can be made in the company and to ensure that the management is keeping shareholder interests in mind while making decisions. The last part has become exceedingly important now with several individuals and groups filing class action lawsuits on firms.

b) Creditors of the firm

Individuals or groups would extend credit to a firm based on their financial strength which is there in the financial statements. This will help them decide on the amount of risk involved in extending credit and accordingly decide on the quantum and period of the credit.

c) Management of the firm

The management might decide targets based on the company's financial statements. These could be in the form of profit growth percentage, sales growth percentage, decrease in the overhead costs etc.

## 1.2 Comment on the below Balance Sheet of a firm

| Assets | | Liabilities | |
|---|---|---|---|
| Cash | $5,000.00 | Long-term loans | $15,000.00 |
| Land | $20,000.00 | Short-term liabilities | $10,000.00 |
| Equipment | $10,000.00 | | |
| Other assets | $1,000.00 | **Equity** | |
| | | Owner's investment | $10,000.00 |
| Total | $36,000.00 | Total | $35,000.00 |

**Solution:**

The above Balance Sheet is incorrect as the Total Assets are not the same as Total Liabilities and Equity. A Balance Sheet should have an exact match between these two totals.

# Practice Exercise

## 1.1 Comment on the below Income Statement

| | | |
|---|---|---|
| Revenues | | $5,000.00 |
| Expenses: | | |
| Cost of raw materials | $3,000.00 | |
| Salaries | $2,000.00 | |
| Interest | $1,000.00 | |
| Income tax | $    - | |
| Total expenses | | $6,000.00 |
| Net Income | | ($1,000.00) |

## 1.2 Why would the following individuals or groups be interested in a firm's financial statements?

a) Prospective shareholders of the firm

b) SEC (Securities and Exchange Commission)

c) Firm's major labor union

This page is intentionally left blank

# Chapter **2**

# Overview of Financial Statements

As mentioned in the previous section, financial statements are made up of three primary items:

a) Balance Sheet,

b) Income Statement and

c) Statement of Cash Flows.

In the below sections we will describe what goes in each of them and their significance.

## Balance Sheet

A balance sheet is a snapshot of a company's source and

application of funds on any given date. Companies prepare a balance sheet every quarter and it reflects the company's state on the last day of the quarter.

There are three items that go in a balance sheet:

a) Assets,

b) Liabilities and

c) Owners' Equity (also called Stockholders' Equity).

Each is described below.

| ASSETS | LIABILITIES |
|---|---|
|  | OWNERS' EQUITY |
| Total Assets = | Total Liabilities and Owners' Equity |

## Assets

These are economic resources of a firm that provide probable future economic benefit due to ownership or control as a result of past transactions or events. Each part of this definition is important. Firstly, "probable benefit" points to a future benefit that ownership of the asset could fetch, like higher sales due to ownership of a machine or new business due to ownership of an office building. Secondly, asset is something that should provide "future economic benefit". This makes anything you own an asset only if it is expected to bring benefit in future, irrespective of past benefits. Finally, "ownership or control as a result of past transactions or events" means that the company should have either ownership or control over the asset to reap the benefit and it will always be due to a past transaction, like buying a building or acquiring an equipment.

Following are some examples of Assets:

a) Cash

b) Accounts Receivable

c) Inventory

d) Prepaid expenses

e) Land

f) Buildings

g) Fixtures and equipment

h) Marketable securities

i) Goodwill (this asset has to be specifically bought in an economic transaction to be recognized as an asset)

Assets appear either on the left-hand side of the balance sheet (in side-by-side format) or at the top (in columnar format). We shall discuss both formats below.

## Liabilities

These are the obligations of economic nature for a firm that might need future sacrifice of benefits of economic nature that are a result of current obligations to give away assets or to provide services to others in future due to past transactions or events. This can be seen as an exact opposite of assets. The "probable future sacrifices" hint towards a payment of some kind that the company would need to make in future, like payment to creditors, bank, suppliers etc. The part about "transfer assets or provide services" refer to an obligation to give up an asset or provide a service, both of which may not be cash transactions but would still consume the company's resources. For example, if a company has sold equipment with a one year warranty, it is obligated to provide service if a fault is detected. This becomes the company's liability. Once again, a liability will be due to "past transactions or events" like assets.

Below are some examples of Liabilities:

a) Short-term loans payable

b) Accounts payable

c) Accrued salaries and wages

d) Long-term notes and debentures

e) Long-term loans payable

Liabilities appear either on the right-hand side of the balance sheet (in side-by-side format) or at the bottom (in columnar format). We shall discuss both formats below.

## Owners' Equity (Stockholders' Equity)

This is the component that belongs to the owners of the company, which includes shareholders. As the company does its business, it either generates profits or incurs losses. Owners' equity increases if it makes profit. If it makes losses, owners' equity reduces. Similarly, if the proprietor withdraws money from the company or the company buys back its own shares then owners' equity reduces. We will see more details about how transactions affect owners' equity in later chapters.

The three predominant components of owners' equity are Paid-in Capital, Retained Earnings and Treasury Stock. These are described below:

## Paid-in Capital

When owners of a company invest cash or other assets in the business, they receive shares of stock in exchange. This gets added to paid-in capital. For example, if a company goes for an IPO (Initial Public Offering) to raise $100 million then once the IPO is over, its paid-in capital would increase by $100 million provided it is able to get full subscription of its new stocks.

It is important to note that when shares are sold in the stock exchange (secondary market), that transaction does not affect owners' equity as it is a market transaction between two investors. The company does not receive anything other than the initial investment when the stock was issued.

## Retained Earnings

This is generally expected to be the largest component of the owners' equity for profitable companies as it reflects the accumulated profits of the company. Each year the company reports either profit or loss in its financial statements. These get added to or subtracted from the retained earnings in the balance sheet. Consider an example where a company starts operations this year and makes a profit of $10,000 this year (this will be shown in the Net Income of the Income Statement). Assuming that the company does not have to pay any dividends, $10,000 will reflect in the Retained Earnings of the Balance Sheet at the end of this year. Now if the company makes a profit of $40,000 next year and, once again, does not pay out any dividend, the Retained Earnings would become $50,000 at the end of the second year. Below sheet shows this condition.

| Income Statement | Year 1 | Year 2 |
|---|---|---|
| Revenues | $50,000 | $250,000 |
| Expenses | $40,000 | $200,000 |
| Net Income | $10,000 | $50,000 |

| Balance Sheet | Year 1 | Year 2 |
|---|---|---|
| Assets | .. | .. |
| Liabilities | .. | .. |
| **Stockholders' Equity** | .. | .. |
| Paid-in Capital | .. | .. |
| Retained Earnings | $10,000 | $60,000 |

## Treasury Stock

Several times highly profitable companies buyback their own shares from the market. This serves two purposes. It is a way the company distributes profits to its shareholders and it sends positive signals about the company's future to the market. When the company does a buy back the treasury stock goes up and that amount gets subtracted from the total owners' equity. Hence, greater the treasury stock, lower the owners' equity. Below is an example.

Number of shares issued (also called outstanding): 10,000

Face value of each share: $1

Hence, Paid-in Capital = $10,000

The Balance Sheet looks as below

| | |
|---|---|
| Assets | $10,000 |
| Total Assets | $10,000 |
| Liabilities | $0 |
| **Stockholders' Equity** | |
| Paid-in Capital | $10,000 |
| Treasury Stock | $0 |
| Total Liabilities and Equity | $10,000 |

Now, let's say that the company decides to buyback 5,000 worth of shares. This will increase the Treasury stock as below. Any increase in Treasury stock is subtracted from the Total Equity as the company has paid money to buy the shares.

| | |
|---|---|
| Assets | $5,000 |
| Total Assets | $5,000 |
| Liabilities | $0 |
| **Stockholders' Equity** | |
| Paid-in Capital | $10,000 |
| Treasury Stock | ($5,000) |
| Total Liabilities and Equity | $5,000 |

It may also be noted that the Assets also reduced by the same amount as Cash, an asset, was used to buyback the shares. This reduces the Total Assets by the same amount as the Treasury Stock.

## Balance Sheet Formats

As stated earlier Balance Sheet has two formats – side-by-side and columnar. The columnar format has an advantage of being able to put figures from previous year for comparison and is hence a preferred way in most cases. Below diagrams show both the formats.

### Side-by-Side Format

| Assets | | Liabilities | |
|---|---|---|---|
| Cash | $500.00 | Short-term loans | $200.00 |
| Land | $400.00 | Bonds | $300.00 |
| | | **Stockholders' Equity** | |
| | | Paid-up capital | $100.00 |
| | | Retained earnings | $ 300.00 |
| Total Assets | $900.00 | Total Liabilities and Stockholders' Equity | $900.00 |

## Columnar Format

| Assets | 2011 | 2010 |
|---|---|---|
| Cash | $500.00 | 400 |
| Land | $400.00 | 300 |
| Total Assets | $900.00 | $700.00 |
| **Liabilities and Stockholders' Equity** | | |
| Short-term loans | $200.00 | $150.00 |
| **Bonds** | **$300.00** | **$300.00** |
| Total Liabilities | $500.00 | $450.00 |
| Paid-up capital | $100.00 | $50.00 |
| Retained earnings | $300.00 | $200.00 |
| Total Stockholders' Equity | $400.00 | $250.00 |
| Total Liabilities and Stockholders' Equity | $900.00 | $700.00 |

# The Accounting Equation

As seen in the previous section, there is a relation between Assets and Liabilities and Stockholders' Equity. This forms the accounting equation and is as given below.

$$Assets = Liabilities + Stockholders'\ Equity$$

OR

$$A = L + E$$

The above relation is always true for any company as assets can be created either through greater liabilities or more investment from stockholders/owners.

# Concepts and Conventions

The Balance Sheet is based on certain concepts and conventions as below:

## Entity Concept

Every corporation is treated as a separate entity, different from other corporations and also different from its owners or shareholders. This means that personal finance activity has to be kept separate from that of the corporation. For example, if the proprietor of a company buys a house, it does not reflect on the financial statement of the company he owns. It is his personal asset. Similarly, if his company buys an office, it will have no change on the proprietor's personal financial statements. This asset will be shown on the company's balance sheet.

## Historical Costs Convention

All assets in the balance sheet are at the value at which they were acquired. For example, land, building and equipment are listed at their buying price, irrespective of their current price. Similarly, the liabilities are also recorded at historical costs. Let's say that a company bought a piece of land for $500,000 in the year 2000. The Balance sheet would show it as an asset worth $50,000. Even though the land value appreciates to $1,000,000 in the year 2010, the company's Balance sheet will show it worth $500,000. This means that the company does not do valuation of its assets every year. All assets are shown as per their original cost price.

## Going Concern

Every balance sheet is prepared on the basis of an assumption that the company will continue to do its business in future. Without this assumption the company would need to re-assess the value of all its assets as if it were going out of business and the balance sheet would look much different. For example, the company could be holding inventory bought at $10,000 but the resale value of that inventory is only $1,000. The company would show the inventory worth $10,000 in its Balance sheet with an assumption that it will continue to do business and use the inventory; it is not going out of business and, hence, does not need to sell its assets right now. It is not liquidating its assets. Without this assumption the company would need to do a revaluation of its assets every quarter/year and that would not be correct as the company is actually not planning to sell them but use them for business purpose.

## Income Statement

An income statement is a statement of the company's revenues and expenses over a period of time – month, quarter, half-year o year. The company's revenue is termed as the "top line" whereas its net income is termed as "bottom line". Both these items are there on the income statement. It may be noted that Income Statement contains values that are to a large extent "estimates" and may not all be "real". All "real" values are present in the statement of cash flows The diagram below shows an Income Statement:

| REVENUES: | $500 |
|---|---|
| EXPENSES: | $300 |
| NET INCOME: | $200 |

## Revenues

Every company operates with an objective of generating money from its business. It achieves this by selling products or services and in doing so generates Revenue. Revenue can take many forms, like sales, licensing, franchising, renting, investing etc. Companies generally use two different heads for revenue. One is for the Sales that form the core business of the company and other is the "Other revenue" that comes from other sources, like interest income, rent etc.

## Expenses

Every company needs to spend money while doing business and generating revenues. This is called Expense, which can take various forms. It can be directly on the product being sold and is called "Cost of Goods Sold". It can also have operating overheads and selling and marketing expenses which are termed as "Selling, General, and Administrative Expenses". Then there are other expenses like Interest expense and Income tax expense.

## Gains and Losses

Sometimes companies may have gains or losses in activities which are not considered as core business activities, like foreign exchange gain/loss or gain/loss from holdings in other companies. Similarly, if a grocery store sells a pickup truck at a profit, it does not reflect in Sales as it is not a gain from its normal business. It is included under the heading Gains and Losses.

## Net Income

This is the difference between the revenues and expenses. If it is negative then there is a net loss. If a company has a net income then it gets added to the retained earnings in the balance sheet after removing any cash dividends. Similarly, a net loss reduces the retained earnings in the balance sheet.

## Dividends

Companies pay out cash dividends to their shareholders. This is a way of sharing profits. However, Dividends do not appear on the Income Statement. They are added after the Income Statement ends (after Net Income). The remaining portion of the Net Income gets added to the Retained Earnings of the Balance Sheet.

## Concepts and Conventions

The Income Statement is based on certain concepts and conventions as below:

### Time Period Concept

An income statement shows the revenues, expenses and net income over a period of time as against the balance sheet, which shows assets, liabilities and stockholders' equity at a particular point of time. Most companies create an income statement at least quarterly. This requires judgment on part of the company's accountants to report partially completed transactions. For example, company's financial statements that are published every quarter will show a period against the Income Statement, whereas, the Balance Sheet will be "as of" a certain date as shown below.

Income Statement from 1st Jan 2011 to 31st Mar 2011

Balance Sheet as on 31st Mar 2011

## Revenue Recognition

There will be transactions that continue for long, starting from order generation to receiving the payment. But this period could see several income statements being created. In such a case it becomes difficult to decide whether the revenue for that transaction should be included (recognized) in the income statement. Following two criteria are used to determine when to recognize revenue:

a) Before recognizing revenue, the promised work must be done, meaning that the goods should have been delivered or the service must have been provided

b) Before recognizing revenue, cash must have been collected, or, at least, collection must be reasonably assured

# Statement of Cash Flows

This is the only statement that contains "real" values of money spent or collected. The only time an entry comes on this statement is when money either goes out from or comes into the account of the organization. The cash items on this statement are divided into three main activities – operating, investing and financing.

The below diagram shows a Statement of Cash Flows

| | |
|---|---|
| Net cash provided by Operating activities: | $500 |
| Net cash used in Investing activities: | ($300) |
| Net cash provided by Financing activities: | $100 |
| Increase in Cash during the year: | $500-$300 + $100 = $300 |

## Operating Activities

All the regular business activities of the business that either use or bring in cash are shown under Cash flow from Operating activities. There would be several entries that would either generate or consume cash and finally provide "Net Cash provided by Operating activities". If this value is negative then the company is utilizing more cash than it is generating from its normal business activities.

## Investing Activities

When a company buys manufacturing equipment, land or building which becomes an asset to help it run its regular business, all these activities are called investing activities. Similarly, sale of land will also be an investing activity that brings in cash. All the inflow and outflow of cash is then netted under the head "Net cash used in Investing activities". This implies that it is expected that a company would have a net cash outflow (a negative value) for this head. This is generally true as these investments add to the company's assets for future benefits.

## Financing Activities

The company borrows money from various sources and also returns them at maturity. All these activities are called financing activities and the head "Net cash provided by Financing activities" shows whether the company has borrowed more than it has returned over the period of time (positive net means the company has borrowed more than it has returned).

In the below example, the company has made cash from operating activities, has a net investment in assets and also a net borrower over the period of time. It can be said that this company is generating cash from its operations and is utilizing a large part of that in investing in assets. Finally, the excess cash from operations and financing increases the cash available with the company (an asset), as seen from "Net increase in cash during the year".

| | | |
|---|---|---|
| Net cash provided by Operating activities | | $5,000.00 |
| **Investing activities:** | | |
| Purchase of property and equipment | ($3,500.00) | |
| Other investments | ($500.00) | |
| Net Cash used in Investing activities | | ($4,000.00) |
| **Financing activities:** | | |
| New bank loans | $1,500.00 | |
| Repayment of old loans | ($500.00) | |
| Payment of cash dividends | ($300.00) | |
| Net cash provided by Financing activities | | $700.00 |
| Net increase in cash during the year | | $1,700.00 |

# Notes to the Financial Statements

Apart from the three main parts of the financial statements, Balance sheet, Income statement and Statement of cash flows, there are a few additional sections. These can be categorized under four general heads as below:

## Summary of Significant Accounting Policies

This section documents the various assumptions, estimates and judgments made in creating the financial statement.

## Additional Information about Summary Totals

Companies summarize several heads under a single summary to

make the financial statement readable. However, each of these summaries could have several items under them which give detailed information to the reader. For example, a single summary called Long-term loans could be broken up into several loans, debentures, bonds with different maturities and amounts.

## Disclosure Information Not Recognized

Revenue recognition concept is applied while compiling the financial statement. But in some cases, like liabilities that could arise due to a lawsuit cannot be recognized. Such items are included in this section. These are also called as contingent liabilities.

## Supplementary Information

These include mandatory information required by FASB and SEC in all financial statements

# Miscellaneous Accounting Concepts and Conventions

Apart from the concepts and conventions that are applied separately to the Balance Sheet and Income Statement, there are certain other concepts and conventions that are applicable to financial statements. These are described below.

## Relevance and Reliability

Financial statements are expected to provide information that is relevant to impact decision making of those who use them.

Similarly, they need to provide reliable data. Sometimes it becomes difficult to arrive at an exact estimate, which can hamper the reliability. In such cases relevance takes precedence and if the data is expected to provide significant information then it is included with estimate based on assumptions.

## Comparability and Consistency

Financial statements should be comparable across companies in the same industry and sometimes, even other industries. This is called comparability. They also need to be consistent in the assumptions and accounting practices over years to compare with previous years' performance. This is called consistency.

## Conservatism

This is a very important concept while recognizing gains and losses. Whenever in doubt, recognize all losses and don't recognize any gains. This gives a pessimistic view to the readers of the financial statements.

## Materiality

An item that can cause significant difference in decision making is called a material item. Special care should be taken while including such items. For example, when a company spends $5 for a pen, it does not matter how the company shows it in their financial statement. But if it spends $5 million in buying a land, it should be included as a separate line item.

## Articulation

The three main parts of the financial statement – Balance Sheet, Income Statement and Statement of cash flows are all closely linked. This should be taken care while preparing them and to not treat them separately but instead, as an integrated set. This relationship, called Articulation, is shown below.

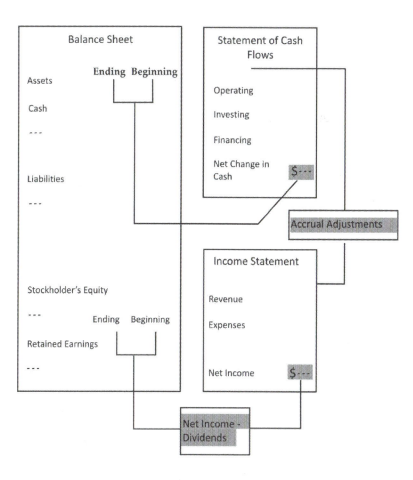

# Solved Examples

**2.1 Classify the following items as assets, liabilities or stockholders' equity.**

**a)** Retained earnings

**b)** Cash

**c)** Land

**d)** Accounts payable

**e)** Accounts receivable

Solution:

a) **Retained earnings** – Stockholders' equity

b) **Cash** – Asset

c) **Land** – Asset

d) **Accounts payable** – Liability

e) **Accounts receivable** – Asset

**2.2 A company's assets are worth $200,000 and its stockholders' equity equals $150,000. What is the amount of its liabilities?**

**Solution:**

As per the accounting equation

Assets = Liabilities + Stockholders' Equity

Hence, Liabilities = Assets – Stockholders' Equity

= $200,000 - $150,000

= $50,000

**2.3 Classify the below items into Balance Sheet and Income Statement items.**

a) Retained earnings

b) Salaries payable

c) Sales

d) Interest earned

e) Land

**Solution:**

a) **Retained earnings** – Balance Sheet as Stockholders' equity

b) **Salaries payable** – Balance Sheet as Liabilities

c) **Sales** – Income Statement

d) **Interest earned** – Income Statement

e) **Land** – Balance Sheet as Asset

**2.4** Using the definition of Asset, choose whether the following form an asset.

a) The company has a legal title to a gold mine. The mine has yielded over $1 million of gold. Company's engineers estimate that no further gold is extractable from the mine.

b) The company is currently negotiating the purchase of a building.

**Solution:**

a) Not an asset as it does not provide any economic benefit in future

b) Not an asset as the company does not yet own it so does not have control over it

**2.5 Using the definition of Liability, choose whether the following are liabilities.**

a) **A company contractually guarantees to replace any of its electronic items sold if they don't work as expected within the first year**

b) **The company estimates the total payroll expenses for the coming year to be $500,000**

**Solution:**

a) A liability as the company is obligated to replace in future due to a past transaction

b) Not a liability as this is not due to a past transaction. This is different than "Salaries payable". Salaries payable means that the employees have already worked but are yet to be paid. In this case the work has not been done yet – it is only estimated.

# Practice Exercise

2.1 Classify the following items as assets, liabilities or stockholders' equity. If any item does not fall in any of these then state the reason for the same.

a) Office equipment

b) Notes payable

c) Firm's good management

d) Office supplies

e) Trademark

f) Notes receivable

2.2 A company's liabilities are worth $250,000 and stockholders' equity worth $500,000. Calculate it total assets.

2.3 ABC Inc. started the month of April with assets worth $1,000,000 and liabilities worth $450,000. During the month of April, stockholders' equity increased by $50,000 and it reduced its liabilities by $40,000. What is the amount of its total assets at the end of April?

2.4 Classify the following into Balance Sheet and Income Statement items.

a) Repairs and maintenance

b) Cost of goods sold

c) Patents

d) Investment in another company

e) Supplies on hand

f) Salary expense

2.5 Identify which of the following transactions would be included in the company's Income Statement.

a) Company borrowed $150,000 from the bank

b) A dividend of $5 per share was declared

c) Cash sales worth $5,000 for the month

d) Collection of $10,000 on account from a credit sales made in the previous month

e) Payment of utility bill worth $500

f) Sales made on account worth $10,000

2.6 Using the definition of Asset, choose whether the following form an asset.

a) The company buys a mining site with an expectation that it has iron ore. It has no other benefit. However, no orehas been found nor is now expected to be present there.

b) The company employs 5 of the world's best engineers recognized in their field

c) The company claims ownership of a large piece of land. Its current market value is $550 million. The government acquired the land for legal reasons and company employees are not allowed to visit the place.

2.7 Using the definition of Liability, choose whether the following form a liability.

a) The company got involved in a lawsuit last year. It lost and was ordered to pay $100 million. It has made the payment.

b) Due to frequent vandalism the company keeps estimates of losses. This year's estimate is that the losses would be worth $1.5 million.

c) The company got services of an accounting firm last year against the obligation to provide them with building security services this year

This page is intentionally left blank

# Chapter **3**

# The Balance Sheet

---

The Balance Sheet contains the company's Assets, Liabilities and Stockholders' Equity. The assets and liabilities are further broken up into short-term (called current) and long-term assets and liabilities. There can be several items under each of these depending upon the company's line of business. Diagram on the following page shows the most common ones.

---

**Balance Sheet**

**Current Assets**

Cash

Accounts Receivable

Inventory

Prepaid Expenses

Investment Securities

**Long-term Assets**

Investments

Property, plant, and equipment

Intangible assets

**Current Liabilities**

Accounts Payable

Accrued Liabilities

Short-term Loans Payable

Current portion of Long-term Debt

**Long-term Liabilities**

Long-term Debt

Deferred Income Tax Liability

**Stockholders' Equity**

Preferred Stock

Common Stock, par value

Additional paid-in Capital

Retained Earnings

Treasury Stock

---

# Current Assets

These are the assets that the company intends to use within one year. Below is a description of the various current assets.

## Cash

Cash refers to the cash-in-hand or in the company's bank accounts. Companies carry cash to take care of daily operational expenses and also to mitigate risk of low sales, slowdown or recession.

## Accounts Receivable

When the company sells products and services to its customers, it may do so without collecting money immediately. The credit period could range from a few days to several months. The amount it expects to receive (within a year) out of the credit extended is shown as a current asset.

## Inventory

Companies maintain an inventory of materials, inventory of in-process items (which are still being manufactured) and an inventory of finished goods until they are sold. The value of these inventories is shown as a current asset at cost price (and not at the selling price) as per accounting guidelines discussed earlier under Historical Costs Convention.

## Prepaid Expenses

Most companies pay several expenses in advance for the entire year or at least for a few months. Most common examples are rent and insurance premiums. Since these are prepaid, they appear as an asset in the Balance Sheet until the year completes, when they get expensed.

## Investment Securities

Companies often park excess cash into short-term investment securities to get higher returns. These are also included in current assets.

## Long-term Assets

These are all those assets that the company plans to hold on to beyond one year. These are made up of a combination of movable and immovable assets. Immovable assets are almost always of a long-term nature.

## Investments

These are similar to investment securities but of a long-term nature. Companies make long-term investments to earn income or to exercise influence over other companies. Whatever be the purpose, as long as the investment is planned to be kept for more than one year, it appears under long-term assets.

## Property, Plant and Equipment (PP and E)

All companies invest in some form of property, plant or equipment. Most of them own an office building or office space. Several manufacturing companies would also own plant (manufacturing plant) and equipment (manufacturing equipment). These kinds of assets are almost always of a long-term nature and hence appear under long-term assets. Plant and equipment have a certain life that could range from a few years to several years. Accordingly, they depreciate in value every year. Hence, the company removes the yearly depreciation on these assets before reporting them on the Balance Sheet. This is called Net value of Plant and Equipment. Depreciation of land is not allowed. Below is an example.

**Property, plant and equipment:**

| | |
|---|---|
| Land | $100,000.00 |
| Buildings | $500,000.00 |
| Furniture and fixtures | $80,000.00 |
| Equipment | $150,000.00 |
| Less accumulated depreciation | ($25,000.00) |
| Total property, plant and equipment, net | $805,000.00 |

## Intangible Assets

The assets like trademark, goodwill, patents etc. are all intangible in nature. But they do provide future benefits and hence should be classified as assets. The challenge is to quantify their value to include in the Balance Sheet. Hence, the rule is to include only those intangible assets for which the company has actually paid money to acquire. For example, if a company buys another company and pays an amount for goodwill, that amount will be shown as an intangible asset under the head goodwill. Intangible assets shed their value over time which is shown under the head Amortization. This concept is similar to depreciation of tangible assets. Hence, the intangible assets, like tangible assets, are shown as net value after subtracting the amortization.

# Current Liabilities

All such liabilities that need to be paid within one year are termed as current liabilities. Below is a description of the most common current liabilities.

## Accounts Payable

This is the amount that the company has to pay to its suppliers for credit granted by them. Credit period depends on the industry and company's relative power over its suppliers. In most cases the credit period is within one year and hence this is shown under current liabilities.

## Accrued Liabilities

Salary to employees is generally paid at the end of the month or twice a month. Similarly, interest on loans is payable once a month or once a quarter. Even though these have not yet been paid they will have to be in the short-term as they have been accrued. Such accrued expenses are captured under accrued liabilities.

## Short-term Loans Payable

Companies wanting money for less than one year may decide to take a short-term loan of a few days up to a year. Since these loans would need to be returned within 1 year they are included under current liabilities.

## Current portion of Long-term Debt

Even long-term debt, like mortgage has monthly payments. All such payments due within one year are classified under current liabilities.

## Long-term Liabilities

All other liabilities that are not maturing within one year are called long-term liabilities. Below is a description of the most common ones.

## Long-term Debt

All companies take long-term loans to finance their long-term investments in property, plant and equipment. These can be in the form of bank loans, long-term bonds, debentures or any other form where a fixed or variable interest is to be paid.

## Deferred Income Tax Liability

Due to government taxation rules, several companies are able to prevent payment of tax immediately. The rules allow them to defer the payment of taxes to a later time. For example, any gain on investment securities is not taxed until the securities are sold even though they have increased in value. Such tax liability is included under long-term liabilities.

# Stockholders' Equity

This is the investment put by the company owners, including stockholders. It also contains the accumulated profits made by the company that belongs to the stockholders. Below are the most common items under this head.

## Preferred Stock

Companies can sell preferred stock that gives fixed returns to stockholders. Hence, it is similar to debt. The only difference between preferred stock and debt is that the prior will not lead the company to bankruptcy if the company is unable to pay the fixed dividend. Preferred stock is different than common stock as the preferred stockholders don't have voting rights. Few companies now issue preferred stocks.

## Common Stock, par value and Additional paid-in Capital

All common stocks have a par value, which is the face value of the stock. Most companies have it as $1 per stock. Hence, if you pay $20 for a stock, you are actually paying $1 for the par value and $19 for additional paid-up capital. When the company issues common stocks for the first time, it may offer them at $10. It will be reflected as below in the Balance Sheet of the company.

**Stockholders' Equity:**

| | |
|---|---|
| Common stock, par value | $1.00 |
| Additional paid-in capital | $19.00 |

After the initial offering when the stocks are traded on the exchange, this transaction will not have any effect on the company's Balance Sheet. For example, if the $20 stock is sold by the initial stockholder to another person for $30, it will only be a profit for the initial stockholder without any bearing on the company's financial statements.

## Retained Earnings

When the company makes a profit, it may pay out some of the profits by way of dividends but retains the rest for investment in assets for further growth. All such profits retained within the company are shown under retained earnings in stockholders' equity. Profits from each year keep adding to the already present retained earnings (a cumulative figure). Similarly, a loss is deducted from the retained earnings and reduces the amount of stockholders' equity.

For example, if the retained earnings are $5,000 and the company has a net income for the year of $500, then the retained earnings become $5,500. Now if the company makes a loss and has a net income of -$100 next year then the retained earnings become $5,400.

## Treasury Stock

Profitable companies also distribute profit to shareholders by buying back their stocks at close to market value (most of the times at a premium above the market value). This reduces the company's number of common stocks outstanding and also reduces the amount of stockholders' equity. Treasury stock is always a negative number and is deducted from the total stockholders' equity.

# Transaction Analysis and Balance Sheet Creation

Every financial transaction needs to reflect in the company's financial statements. But the Balance Sheet contains only a few summarized heads which are shown. Hence, putting a transaction under the correct head(s) is important to be able to prepare a Balance Sheet. Below is a template showing some of the common heads under Assets, Liabilities and Stockholders' equity that needs to be used for doing transaction analysis. Additional heads can also be added at appropriate places as needed. It should be noted that for every transaction the accounting equation, Assets = Liabilities + Stockholders' Equity, should hold true. If it does not, then the transaction has been incorrectly recorded.

The three transactions described in the above sheet are as follows:

| | Transaction 1 | Transaction 2 | Transaction 3 | Total |
|---|---|---|---|---|
| Cash | $500.00 | ($200.00) | $1,000.00 | $1,300.00 |
| Inventory | | | | $0.00 |
| Prepaid expenses | | | | $0.00 |
| Property, plant and equipment | | $5,000.00 | | $5,000.00 |
| Total Assets | $500.00 | $4,800.00 | $1,000.00 | $6,300.00 |
| Accounts payable | | $4,800.00 | | $4,800.00 |
| Long-term debt | | | $1,000.00 | $1,000.00 |
| Paid-in Capital | $500.00 | | | $500.00 |
| Total Liabilities and Equity | $500.00 | $4,800.00 | $1,000.00 | $6,300.00 |

## Transaction 1

Company issues stocks worth $500 and receives that money in cash. This increases the cash asset by $500 and also the paid-in capital by $500.

## Transaction 2

The company buys property, plant and equipment worth $5,000. It pays only $200 from its cash and agrees to pay the rest on credit later on. This reduces the cash asset by $200 and increases the long-term asset (property, plant and equipment) by $5,000. It also increases the current liability, accounts payable, by $4,800 – the amount of credit the company has taken on this purchase.

## Transaction 3

The company decides to take a long-term loan from the bank worth $1,000. This increases its cash asset by $1,000 and increases its long-term debt liability by the same amount.

It may be noted that for each transaction the "Total Assets" column is exactly equal to the "Total Liabilities and Equity" column. It may also be noted that the final value of "Total Assets" is also equal to the final value of "Total Liabilities and Equity". Both of these should always occur for the transactions to have been noted correctly.

The information from the transaction analysis can now be used to create a Balance Sheet as below

|  | **Balance Sheet** |
| --- | --- |
|  | **January 1, 2011** |
| **Current assets:** | |
| Cash | $1,300.00 |
| **Long-term assets:** | |
| Property, plant and equipment | $5,000.00 |
| Total assets | $6,300.00 |
| **Current liabilities:** | |
| Accounts payable | $4,800.00 |
| **Long-term liabilities:** | |
| Long-term debt | $1,000.00 |
| Total liabilities | $5,800.00 |
| **Stockholders' equity:** | |
| Paid-in capital | $500.00 |
| Total liabilities and equity | $6,300.00 |

## Solved Examples

**3.1 Classify the below transactions into the following**

a) Current assets

b) Long-term investments

c) Property, plant and equipment

d) Intangible assets

e) Current liabilities

f) Long-term liabilities

g) Stockholders' equity

h) Not a balance sheet item

Transactions:

   i. Inventory

  ii. Current portion of long-term debt

 iii. Sales

 iv. Stock of another company

   v. Land

 vi. Accounts payable

vii. Bonds payable

Solution:

   i. **Inventory** – Current assets

  ii. **Current portion of long-term debt** – Current liabilities

 iii. **Sales** – Not a balance sheet item

 iv. **Stock of another company** – Long-term investment

   v. **Land** – Property, plant and equipment

 vi. **Accounts payable** – Current liabilities

vii. **Bonds payable** – Long-term liabilities

**3.2** On Jan 1ˢᵗ, 2011, the first day of business for ABC Inc., it entered into the following transactions:

a) Initial cash investment by stockholders - $150,000

b) Purchased equipment for $100,000 in cash

c) Traded the equipment for a piece of land worth $60,000. Also received $40,000 cash in the trade.

d) Borrowed $150,000 cash from the bank at 9% interest rate. Principle and interest are to be paid after four months.

e) Issued $200,000 in bonds in exchange for cash. Interest rate is 10% paid semi-annually. Bonds are for 25 years.

f) ABC Inc. re-purchased some of the stocks for $40,000

g) Purchased a building and some equipment for $300,000 in cash. Cost of equipment alone is $190,000.

Analyze the above transaction and put them in the analysis sheet shown earlier. Prepare a balance sheet for ABC Inc. at the end of Jan 1ˢᵗ, 2011.

Solution:

| | i | ii | iii | iv | v | vi | vii | Total |
|---|---|---|---|---|---|---|---|---|
| Cash | $150,000 | ($100,000) | $40,000 | $150,000 | $200,000 | ($40,000) | ($300,000) | $100,000 |
| Equipment | | $100,000 | ($100,000) | | | | $190,000 | $190,000 |
| Land and Building | | | $60,000 | | | | $110,000 | $170,000 |
| Total Assets | $150,000 | $0 | $0 | $150,000 | $200,000 | ($40,000) | $0 | $460,000 |
| Bonds | | | | | $200,000 | | | $200,000 |
| Bank Loan | | | | $150,000 | | | | $150,000 |
| Paid-in Capital | $150,000 | | | | | | | $150,000 |
| Treasury stock | | | | | | ($40,000) | | |
| Total Liabilities and Equity | $150,000 | $0 | $0 | $150,000 | $200,000 | ($40,000) | $0 | $460,000 |

a) This is a purely financing transaction of issuing stocks worth $150,000

b) This is buying of equipment for cash

c) This transaction involves buying an asset for another + cash

d) This is a financing transaction. Since this is a new loan, there is no interest liability yet.

e) This is also a financing transaction. Since this is new bond, there is no interest liability yet.

f) This is re-purchase of shares that reduces the stockholders' equity

g) This transaction involves upfront buying of building and equipment with cash

Below is the balance sheet of the company at the end of the day

**ABC Inc.**
**Balance Sheet**
**January 1, 2011**

| | |
|---|---|
| **Current assets:** | |
| Cash | $100,000 |
| **Long-term assets**: | |
| Equipment | $190,000 |
| Land and Building | $170,000 |
| Total assets | $460,000 |
| **Current liabilities:** | |
| Bank Loan | $200,000 |
| **Long-term liabilities:** | |
| Bonds | $150,000 |
| Total liabilities | $350,000 |
| **Stockholders' equity:** | |
| Paid-in capital | $150,000 |
| Treasury stock | ($40,000) |
| Total liabilities and equity | $460,000 |

**3.3 Following items are available for the company's fixed assets. Compute the values that will be shown in the balance sheet.**

| | |
|---|---|
| Land | $100,000 |
| Building | $500,000 |
| Equipment | $250,000 |
| Accumulated depreciation – building | $200,000 |
| Accumulated depreciation – equipment | $100,000 |

### Solution:

Balance sheet shows the net value of the assets. In the above case, Land will be shown at its original value, whereas, building and equipment will be netted by removing the depreciation and shown as below.

**Property and equipment:**

| | |
|---|---|
| Land | $100,000 |
| Building | $500,000 |
| Equipment | $250,000 |
| Less accumulated depreciation | ($300,000) |
| Total property and equipment, net | $550,000 |

# Practice Exercise

**3.1 Classify the below transactions into the following**

a) Current assets

b) Long-term investments

c) Property, plant and equipment

d) Intangible assets

e) Current liabilities

f) Long-term liabilities

g) Stockholders' equity

h) Not a balance sheet item

Transactions

    i. Rent expense

   ii. Note receivable, due in 5 years

  iii. Additional paid-in capital

  iv. Retained earnings

   v. Short-term interest earning securities

  vi. Copyright owned by firm

 vii. Cars used for business

viii. Prepaid insurance

  ix. Accumulated depreciation

   x. Common stock

**3.2 Prepare a balance sheet using the following balances**

| | |
|---|---|
| Cash in bank accounts | $42,000 |
| Accounts receivable | $55,000 |
| Inventory | $88,000 |
| Investment in 2-month US Treasury securities | $30,000 |
| Long-term investment | $10,000 |
| Land and Building | $300,000 |
| Accumulated depreciation – building | $27,000 |
| Equipment | $64,000 |
| Accumulated depreciation – equipment | $10,000 |
| Patent | $18,000 |
| Long-term note receivable | $16,000 |
| Accounts payable | $66,000 |
| Current portion of long-term debt | $72,000 |
| Long-term debt | $100,000 |
| Common stock, par value | $40,000 |
| Additional paid-in capital | $200,000 |
| Retained earnings | Need to compute |

3.3 On Jan 1$^{st}$, 2011, its first day of business, XYZ Inc., entered into the following transactions:

a) Initial cash investment by stockholders worth $880,000

b) Purchased equipment for $200,000 in cash

c) Borrowed $640,000 from the bank at 6% interest rate for 3 years

d) Bought a building for $2,000,000. Paid $800,000 in cash and the rest on mortgage at 5%. Interest is payable yearly and the term of loan is 10 years.

e) Purchased inventory for $180,000 on account

f) Paid $12,000 for fire insurance of the building for the entire year

g) Paid off $60,000 for the credit on inventory purchased earlier

Analyze the above transaction using the analysis sheet. Prepare a balance sheet at the end of Jan 1st, 2011.

## 3.4 Prepare a balance sheet using the below items

| | |
|---|---|
| Accounts payable | $39,000 |
| Accounts receivable | $51,250 |
| Accumulated depreciation – building | $50,000 |
| Accumulated depreciation – equipment | $6,250 |
| Building | $250,000 |
| Cash | $40,000 |
| Cash for long-term use in restricted account | $12,500 |
| Common stock, par value | $25,000 |
| Equipment | $100,000 |
| Inventory | $50,000 |
| Long-term investment | $12,500 |
| Interest payable | $8,750 |
| Land | $125,000 |
| Long-term note payable | $75,000 |
| Investment securities | $6,250 |
| Retained earnings | $192,500 |
| Short-term loan payable | $26,000 |
| Additional paid-in capital | $225,000 |

# Chapter **4**

# The Income Statement

Income statement contains the revenue and expenses transactions over a period of time – generally a quarter or year. A balance sheet is a snapshot, whereas, an income statement is a running log. Like different types of assets and liabilities on the balance sheet, there are different kinds of revenues and expenses on the income statement. There are also several interim values in the income statement that carry importance. Below diagram shows all the major terms in an income statement.

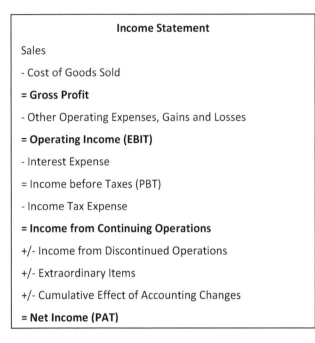

**Income Statement**

Sales

- Cost of Goods Sold

**= Gross Profit**

- Other Operating Expenses, Gains and Losses

**= Operating Income (EBIT)**

- Interest Expense

= Income before Taxes (PBT)

- Income Tax Expense

**= Income from Continuing Operations**

+/- Income from Discontinued Operations

+/- Extraordinary Items

+/- Cumulative Effect of Accounting Changes

**= Net Income (PAT)**

# Measures of Income

As seen in the above diagram, there are various ways using which one can measure a company's income. Each of them conveys different information about a company's revenue and expenses. Below is a description of these measures.

## Gross Profit

For a company selling products gross profit is the difference between the selling price and the cost price of the product. For example, for a car manufacturer, gross profit is the difference between the price of the car at which the company sells to the dealer and the cost of manufacturing it. Similarly, for a grocery store, it is the difference between the price at which the store sells groceries and the wholesale cost at which it buys it.

## Operating Income (EBIT)

Every company has overheads related to administrative, selling, marketing, and other functions. When all these are removed from the gross profit, we get another important measure of profit called Operating Income or Earnings before Interest and Tax (EBIT).

## Income (Profit) before Taxes (PBT)

Companies that have any kind of debt financing have an interest expense to pay. They can be bank loans, bonds, preferred stock, or any other such financing that pays interest. The only financing that does not have interest payments is common equity. When the interest expense is subtracted from EBIT, we get Income before Taxes or Profit before Taxes (PBT).

## Income from Continuing Operations

After removing the income tax expense we get the bottom line called as Income from Continuing Operations. The items that this profit measure does not include are called "below the line items" – Income from discontinued operations, extraordinary items and cumulative effect of accounting changes.

## Below the Line Items

Income from Discontinued Operations is reported when the revenue is generated by a part of business that is being discontinued. For example, when a retail chain plans to close a store in the year, it will report revenue from that store under this head.

Extraordinary Items are those items that are one time in nature and the company does not expect to see them on a regular basis in future. For example, a big loss due to a natural disaster like fire or earthquake would be shown under this head.

Cumulative Effect of Accounting Changes refers to any changes in the income due to change in the assumptions made while making the financial statements and, hence, are not considered to be a regular business income or expense.

## Net Income (PAT)

In most cases the Net Income or Profit after Tax (PAT) will be same as Income from Continuing Operations as the "below the line items" are not always present. This is the final measure of profit and this is what is seen by most companies, investors and analysts while analyzing a company's profitability.

# Types of Revenues

Although we have shown revenue as a single item in the above example Income Statement, it can be from several sources. Accordingly, we may show them separately as several items. Below are the most common sources of revenue.

## Sales Revenue

This revenue is generated when a company sells its products. For example, an automobile company generates sales revenue when it sells its cars.

## Service Revenue

Companies in the services business generate revenue under this head by selling services. For example, an accounting firm generates this revenue through its consulting business.

## Interest Revenue

This revenue can be a small component for some companies who have simply parked extra cash to generate some interest income. However, this could be a major source of revenue for banks.

# Types of Expenses

As there are several streams of revenue, there are also several streams of expenses. Below is a description of the most commonly found expenses.

## Cost of Goods Sold

This is the cost of manufacturing of the product that is sold by a company. For a car manufacturer, this is how much it costs to build a car and for a retailer this is the wholesale cost of its apparels.

## Selling, General, and Administrative Expenses

These are all the expenses that are incurred in the administrative, sales and marketing work in the company that cannot be directly tied to any particular sale. These are mostly the indirect expenses of the company.

## Research and Development Expense

Although R and D brings about future benefits, it is not reported as an asset. This is because it is difficult to estimate the value it can bring in future and hence leaves a lot to individual judgment. Hence, this expense is reported in the income statement under R and D expense head.

## Wages and Salary Expense

This includes all payroll related expenses, including all employee benefits, pensions, healthcare etc.

## Bad Debt Expense

When some debtors do not pay the company, partly or fully, that amount is reported under this head in the income statement.

## Depreciation

Buildings and equipment are allowed to depreciate over a period of time based on their expected life as discussed in the previous chapter. This means that they are depreciated every year until they are totally consumed. Each year the depreciation is calculated and reported in the income statement and also subtracted from the gross value of Property, plant and equipment in the balance sheet to give a net value of Property, plant and equipment.

Depreciation is done using one of two methods – straight-line depreciation method and double declining-balance method. In straight-line depreciation, the depreciation every year is equal over the life of the asset. In double declining-balance method it is higher in the early years and reduces later on. Below is an example of an asset with the cost of $40,000 with life of five years.

Cost = $40,000

Residual value = $4,000 (estimated resale value expected after 5 years)

Useful life = 5 years

Straight Line depreciation = (Cost – Residual value)/Useful life = ($40,000 - $4,000)/5 = $7,200

Double declining-balance depreciation = Book Value * Fixed percentage every year

For year 1 with 40%, it will be = $40,000 * 0.4 = $16,000

For year 2 with 40%, it will be = ($40,000 - $16,000) * 0.4 = $9,600

The depreciation under the two types would look like below:

| Year | Depreciation | | Accumulated Depreciation | | Book Value | |
|---|---|---|---|---|---|---|
| | Straight Line | Double declining-balance | Straight Line | Double declining-balance | Straight Line | Double declining-balance |
| 1 | $7,200 | $16,000 | $7,200 | $16,000 | 32,800 | $24,000 |
| 2 | $7,200 | $9,600 | $14,400 | $25,600 | $25,600 | $14,400 |
| 3 | $7,200 | $5,760 | $21,600 | $31,360 | $18,400 | $8,640 |
| 4 | $7,200 | $3,456 | $28,800 | $34,816 | $11,200 | $5,184 |
| 5 | $7,200 | $1,184 | $36,000 | $36,000 | $4,000 | $4,000 |

In the last year, the depreciation under double declining-balance would be equal to whatever is remaining over and above the residual value of $4,000.

## Interest Expense

This is the amount of money the company pays for its debt and preferred stock

## Income Tax Expense

This is the amount of money the company needs to pay to government by way of income tax

# Earnings per Share (EPS)and Diluted EPS

This is a very important measure shown on the Income Statement after the Net Income. It is calculated by dividing Net Income by Total Number of Common Stock of the company. It gives an idea of how much value the company has added in the year per share.

There is also another measure called, Diluted Earnings per Share (Diluted EPS) which is mentioned below EPS. If the company has pledged stock options to its employees or others then it takes those into account while calculating Diluted EPS.

For example, if the company's Net Income is $500 and it has 500 shares outstanding, then it's EPS = $1. But if the company also has pledged stock options of 100 shares to its employees then it's Diluted EPS = 0.833 ($500/600).

# Revenue Recognition

Consider an example that you have sold some product to a customer who will pay after three months. Should you recognize revenue now or three months later? Similarly, consider receiving an advance payment for work that is to be done after one month.

Should the revenue be recognized now or after one month? In order to answer the above questions, there are two criteria that help determine when to recognize revenue. They are as below:

a) The promised work must be done before revenue is recognized

b) Cash collection should be reasonably assured before revenue is recognized

As per the above criteria, revenue should not be recognized before the work is completed but can be before money is collected, as long as it is assured. Below are some examples of revenue recognition.

A grocery store sells items for immediate cash payment. Hence, revenue is recognized as soon as a sale is made.

Some retailers allow a credit period when customers buy home appliances. In such a case even though the goods are delivered, money is not paid immediately. In such cases the retailer has two options. Either to recognize the revenue immediately if the payment is assured or recognize in parts as the payment is made.

An airlines company asks flyers to pay for their ticket in advance when booking even though the flight is actually after a few months. In this case the airline does not recognize revenue until it has actually completed the work of transporting the customer.

Football season tickets are paid for in advance but revenue is recognized gradually as the season progresses

Software product vendors sell their software along with 1 year warranty support. Hence, they recognize some part of the revenue at sale time and the rest over a period of time as the support nears its end.

## Expense Recognition

As we saw above, revenue is recognized based on the two criteria explained above. The expense incurred to provide that product or service also needs to follow some rules to ensure that it gets recognized along with the revenue. If this does not happen, then the net income calculation might be incorrect. In most cases the "matching concept" is used to recognize expense. This means that the expense is matched with revenue and recognized together. This makes sense for direct expenses but cannot be used with overheads, like sales and promotion expenses. These expenses are recognized immediately as they cannot be matched directly with any revenue. Yet another way of recognizing revenue is depreciation. Capital equipment and building depreciate over a period of time and this depreciation is carried in pre-determined instalments every year in the income statement. This is again because their expense cannot be directly matched with revenue nor should they be immediately expensed as they become the company's asset. Below are the three ways:

a)  Direct matching, as with cost of goods sold

b)  Immediate recognition, as with advertising

c)  Systematic allocation, as with depreciation

## Expanded Accounting Equation

As seen above, the accounting equation goes as below:

Assets = Liabilities + Equity

However, Equity = Paid-in capital + Retained earnings

Now, Retained earnings gets computed on the basis of how much profit or loss the company makes. In the previous chapter we have seen that, Retained earnings = Net income – Dividends.

This can be further broken up into,

Retained earnings = (Revenues – Expenses) – Dividends

So, we finally have,

**Equity = Paid-in capital + (Revenues – Expenses) – Dividends**

This is the expanded form of the accounting equation.

The next section shows transaction analysis using this expanded equation.

## Transaction Analysis and Income Statement Creation

The below transaction sheet template can be used for analyzing financial transactions and it finally helps prepare an Income Statement. It is similar to the one used earlier for preparing a Balance Sheet with three additions – Revenue, Expenses and Dividends. Please note that some of the heads under assets have been omitted to make the sheet fit on the page. Similarly, all the revenue streams – sales revenue, services revenue and interest revenue are clubbed together into a single head called Revenue to save space. All expenses are also clubbed together under a general Expense head. In reality they can be Cost of Goods Sold, Interest expense, Wages, Depreciation etc.

| | Transaction 1 | Transaction 2 | Transaction 3 | Total |
|---|---|---|---|---|
| Cash | $1,000.00 | ($200.00) | ($250.00) | $550.00 |
| Inventory | ($700.00) | | | ($700.00) |
| Total Assets | $300.00 | ($200.00) | ($250.00) | ($150.00) |
| Accounts payable | | | | $0.00 |
| Long-term debt | | | | $0.00 |
| Paid in capital | | | | $0.00 |
| Revenue | $1,000.00 | | | $1,000.00 |
| Expense | ($500.00) | ($200.00) | | ($700.00) |
| Dividends | | | ($250.00) | ($250.00) |
| Total Liabilities and Equity | $500.00 | ($200.00) | ($250.00) | $50.00 |

The three transactions described in the above sheet are as follows:

## Transaction 1

Company sells goods worth $500 for $1,000. This results in $1,000 revenue. Applying the matching concept, the expense of $500 is immediately applied. This expense is actually Cost of Goods Sold. Due to this transaction, the company also receives $1,000 in cash and its inventory reduces by $500. It is important to note here that the reduction in inventory should match the Cost of Goods Sold expense as inventory is shown at cost price.

## Transaction 2

This is a transaction where the company pays out interest on its loans. The $200 expense is actually Interest expense. It also reduces the cash by an equal amount.

## Transaction 3

In this transaction the company pays out $250 dividend to its shareholders. This also reduces the cash by an equal amount.

It may again be noted that in each of the above transactions the expanded accounting equation holds true. The income statement based on the above transactions is as below.

**Income Statement**
**Revenue:**
| | | |
|---|---|---|
| Sales | | $1,000.00 |

**Expenses:**
| | | |
|---|---|---|
| Cost of goods sold | $500.00 | |
| Interest expense | $200.00 | |
| | | $700.00 |
| Net Income | | $300.00 |
| Dividends | | $250.00 |

It should be noted that although Dividends are shown in the above income statement, they are actually not a part of the income statement. The income statement ends at Net Income. Dividends are mentioned after that to provide enough information about retained earnings.

# Solved Examples

**4.1 Classify the below items under the following heads found in the Income Statement.**

a) Revenue

b) Cost of goods sold

c) Selling, general, and administrative expense

d) Other income statement item

e) Not an income statement item

The items to classify are as below.

   i. Prepaid insurance

  ii. Restructuring charge

 iii. Interest payable

  iv. Sales

   v. Gain on sale of land

  vi. Taxes payable

 vii. Advertising expense

**Solution:**

   i. **Prepaid insurance** – Not an income statement item. This is an asset in the balance sheet.

  ii. **Restructuring charge** – Other income statement item

 iii. **Interest payable** – Not an income statement item. This is a liability in the balance sheet.

  iv. **Sales** – Revenue

   v. **Gain on sale of land** – Other income statement item. Comes under Gains and Losses.

  vi. **Taxes payable** – Not an income statement item. This is a liability in the balance sheet.

vii. **Advertising expense** – Selling, general, and administrative expense

**4.2 Indicate whether the following items fall under Revenue, Expense, Gain or Loss.**

a) Interest earned on short-term investment

b) Retail price of goods sold

c) Fees received in exchange for providing a service

d) Wholesale cost of goods sold

**Solution:**

a) **Interest earned on short-term investment** – Revenue

b) **Retail price of goods sold** – Revenue. This is the selling price.

c) **Fees received in exchange for providing a service** – Revenue

d) **Wholesale cost of goods sold** – Expense. This is the cost of goods sold.

**4.3** XYZ Inc. has the following transactions in 2011. Prepare an Income Statement for the firm.

a) Insurance expense $15,000

b) Advertising expense $60,000

c) Salary and wages $100,000

d) Equipment rental revenue $600,000

e) Interest earned on idle cash $2,000

f) Other expenses $45,000

g) Rental revenue for idle warehouse $40,000

h) Income tax expense @25% of income before taxes

The company also has 1,000,000 common shares outstanding. Calculate the EPS.

**Solution:**

The Income Statement should have all the revenues on top followed by all the expenses. However, we would first need to compute the Profit before Tax (PBT) and then calculate the Income Tax expense. We would finally get the Net Income or Profit after Tax (PAT).

**XYZ Inc.**

## Income Statement for 2011

**Revenues:**

| | |
|---|---|
| Equipment rental revenue | $600,000.00 |
| Warehouse rental revenue | $40,000.00 |
| Interest revenue | $2,000.00 |
| Total revenues | $642,000.00 |

**Expenses:**

| | |
|---|---|
| Salary and Wages | $100,000.00 |
| Insurance expense | $15,000.00 |
| Advertising expense | $ 60,000.00 |
| Other expenses | $45,000.00 |
| Total expenses | $220,000.00 |
| Profit before Tax | $422,000.00 |
| Income Tax @25% | $105,500.00 |
| Net Income | $316,500.00 |
| Common shares outstanding | 1,000,000.00 |
| EPS | $0.3165 |

**4.4 XYZ Inc. has begun the year with the following account balances:**

| | |
|---|---|
| Cash | $5,000 |
| Accounts receivable | $14,000 |
| Inventory | $11,000 |
| Accounts payable | $8,000 |
| Paid-in capital | $7,000 |
| Retained earnings | $15,000 |

During the year the following transactions took place. Use the transaction analysis worksheet and prepare the Income Statement and Balance Sheet for the company.

a) Sales of $225,000, 90% on account

b) Cash collections on receivable of $200,000

c) Purchased inventory on account for $180,000

d) Cost of inventory sold $175,000

e) Paid accounts payable $173,000

f) Paid misc expenses $37,000

Solution:

Below analysis sheet shows the above transactions

| | Opening Balance | i | ii | iii | iv | v | vi | Total |
|---|---|---|---|---|---|---|---|---|
| Cash | $5,000 | $22,500 | $200,000 | | | ($173,000) | ($37,000) | $17,500 |
| Accounts receivable | $14,000 | $202,500 | ($200,000) | | | | | $16,500 |
| Inventory | $11,000 | | | $180,000 | ($175,000) | | | $16,000 |
| Total Assets | $30,000 | $225,000 | $0 | $180,000 | ($175,000) | ($173,000) | ($37,000) | $50,000 |
| Accounts payable | $8,000 | | | $180,000 | | ($173,000) | | $15,000 |
| Paid-in Capital | $7,000 | | | | | | | $7,000 |
| Retained earnings | $15,000 | | | | | | | $15,000 |
| Sales | | $225,000 | | | | | | $225,000 |
| Cost of goods sold | | | | | ($175,000) | | | ($175,000) |
| Misc expense | | | | | | | ($37,000) | ($37,000) |
| Total Liabilities and Equity | $30,000 | $225,000 | $0 | $180,000 | ($175,000) | ($173,000) | ($37,000) | $50,000 |

The company's Income Statement is as below

**XYZ Inc.**

**Income Statement for 2011**

**Revenues:**

| | |
|---|---|
| Sales | $225,000.00 |
| Total revenues | $225,000.00 |

**Expenses:**

| | |
|---|---|
| Cost of goods sold | $175,000.00 |
| Misc expenses | $ 37,000.00 |
| Total expenses | $212,000.00 |

| | |
|---|---|
| Net Income | $13,000.00 |

The company's Balance Sheet is as below

**XYZ Inc.**

**Balance Sheet**

**January 1, 2011**

| | |
|---|---|
| **Current assets:** | |
| Cash | $17,500 |
| Accounts receivable | $16,500 |
| Inventory | $16,000 |
| Total assets | $50,000 |
| **Current liabilities:** | |
| Accounts payable | $15,000 |
| Total liabilities | $15,000 |
| **Stockholders' equity:** | |
| Paid-in capital | $7,000 |
| Retained earnings* | $28,000 |
| Total liabilities and equity | $50,000 |

Retained earnings is a cumulative figure. Last year it was $15,000. This year the Net Income will be added to it to make it $28,000.

Below is the formula.

Retained earnings (2011) = Retained earnings (2010) + Net Income (2011) – Dividends (2011)

# Practice Exercise

**4.1** Classify the below items under the following heads found in the Income Statement.

a) Revenue

b) Cost of goods sold

c) Selling, general, and administrative expense

d) Other income statement item

e) Not an income statement item

The items to classify are as below.

   i. Delivery expense

  ii. Income tax expense

 iii. CEO's salary

 iv. Dividends paid

   v. Sales commission paid

 vi. Supplies on hand

 vii. Gain on sale of land

viii. Depreciation expense

**4.2** Indicate whether the following items fall under Revenue, Expense, Gain or Loss.

a) Sale of delivery truck for more than its purchase price

b) Sale of land for less than its purchase price

c) Estimated amount of accounts receivable created this year that will be uncollectible

d) Destruction of warehouse in fire

4.3 XYZ Inc. has the following transactions in 2011. Prepare an Income Statement for the firm.

a) Sales worth $200,000

b) All items were priced at 1.25 times their cost

c) Salary and wages were 5% of sales

d) Insurance expense $2,000

e) Other expenses were 1% of cost of goods sold

f) Advertising and promotion expense were 2% of sales

g) Income tax expense @30% of income before taxes

The company also has 500,000 common shares outstanding. Calculate the EPS.

4.4 ZZZ company begun the year with the following balances:

| | |
|---|---|
| Cash | $15,000 |
| Accounts receivable | $42,000 |
| Inventory | $33,000 |
| Accounts payable | $24,000 |
| Paid-in capital | $45,000 |
| Retained earnings | $21,000 |

The following transaction took place during the year. Analyze them using the transaction analysis sheet and prepare the company's Income Statement and Balance Sheet.

a) Borrowed $30,000 on a long term loan

b) Interest expense for the year $3,000. This amount has not yet been paid.

c) Sales for the year was $500,000, all on account

d) Cash collections on account receivable $280,000

e) Purchased inventory on account $380,000

f) Cost of inventory sold was $350,000

g) Paid accounts payable $173,000

h) Paid wage expense $137,000

# Chapter **5**

# The Statement of Cash Flows

Values that go in the Balance Sheet and Income statement are estimates based on some underlying assumptions. Hence, they may not give the right picture. As against this, the statement of cash flows is completely realistic. It shows how much cash comes in and goes out of the company's bank accounts. It does not have any assumptions. Hence, it gives a more realistic picture of how a company is doing.

## Categories of Cash Flow Activities

Both Balance Sheet and Income Statement contain one single figure, like Total Assets, Total Liabilities and Equity, or Net

Income that is generally looked at. However, Cash Flow statement contains three independent items that are looked at. They fall under the following categories:

a) Operating activities

b) Investing activities

c) Financing activities

All financial transactions that involve a cash flow (not on credit) are classified in one of these categories. They are, accordingly, placed in separate parts of the statement of cash flows and have separate significance. Below sections describe each of these categories.

## Operating Activities

Any cash inflow or outflow from the company's regular business activities is called Operating cash flow. This includes cash collected from customers from selling of goods or services and cash paid to suppliers and employees for their goods and services. Cash inflows from interest and dividend income due to the company's investments also fall under this category. Operating activities are all those activities that are related to current assets and liabilities, except those liabilities which are related to financing, like loans. Below activities fall under Operating activities.

**Cash inflow:**
Sale of goods or services
Sale of trading securities
Interest revenue
Dividend revenue

**Cash outflow:**
Inventory purchases
Wages and salaries
Taxes
Interest expense
Other expenses (utility bills, rent etc.)
Purchase of trading securities

## Investing Activities

Companies invest in long-term assets like property, plant, and equipment, long-term investment in other companies and giving out loans to other companies. All activities related to these investing activities are the Investing cash flow. Below are the activities under Investing activities.

**Cash inflow:**
Sale of plant
Sale of land or building
Sale of equipment
Sale of business segment
Sale of non-trading securities
Collection of principal on loans

**Cash outflow:**
Purchase of plant
Purchase of land or building
Purchase of equipment
Purchase of non-trading securities
Extending loans to other entities

## Financing Activities

Companies finance using various means, like common stock, preferred stock and debt. They may also pay cash dividends to shareholders. All of these financing activities are seen under Financing cash flow. It is worth noting that cash dividends paid by the company are part of financing activities, whereas, interest expense is part of operating activities. Below are all the financing activities.

**Cash inflow:**
Issuance of common stock
Issuance of preferred stock
Debt (loans, bonds, notes mortgages etc.)

**Cash outflow:**
Cash dividends
Repayment of debt
Repurchase of stock (treasury stock)

# Cash Flow Pattern

The normal pattern of net cash flow for a company is as below:

   a) Net cash inflow from Operating activities +

   b) Net cash outflow in Investing activities -

   c) Net cash inflow/outflow from Financing activities +/-

Positive cash flow from operation is especially important for all companies except for start-ups. Cash outflow into investing activities is generally seen in companies as they create assets for future growth. Depending upon whether a company is able to finance all its investments using its operating cash flow or not, its cash flow from financing activities will be either positive or negative.

Below is a typical cash flow for companies at various stages

## Start-up Company

Since these companies don't have much business, most of their cash flow needs are from financing activities, which feed into both operating and investment needs.

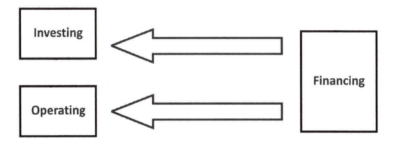

## Steady-state Company

A well settled company generates enough cash from operations to use the cash in investing and also to pay dividends for common and preferred stocks.

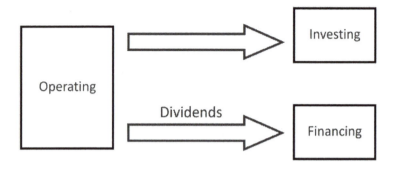

## Cash Cow

A cash cow is a company that generates enough cash to use in investing and for repayment of loans, share re-purchases and payment of dividends.

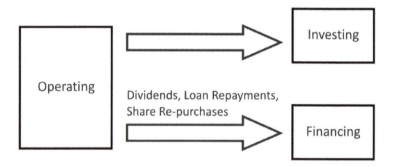

## Cash Flow Statement Preparation

The statement of cash flows can be prepared using two different methods:

a)  Direct method and

b)  Indirect method.

Direct method uses transaction analysis in the same way as was done for preparing balance sheet and income statement. However, it is a less common method. Most companies create it using the indirect method. Below are the two methods.

## Direct Method

All the transactions are analyzed and the ones involving cash inflow or outflow are captured and put in the statement of cash flows as below.

Transactions:

1. Sales on account for $10,000
2. Collections on account for $12,000
3. Purchased inventory on account for $8,000
4. Cost of goods sold is $8,000
5. Paid accounts payable worth $7,500
6. Purchased property, plant, and equipment worth $4,000
7. Sold property, plant, and equipment for $1,500 cash
8. Repaid a bank loan worth $500
9. Issued new stock worth $1,000 and collected cash
10. Depreciation expense of $400
11. Interest payment of $250 in cash
12. Interest accrued is worth $50
13. Wages and supplies expenses worth $1,500 paid in cash
14. Recorded income tax expense of $500
15. Paid income tax of $400

Below table splits the above transactions into cash and non-cash. It also classifies the cash transactions into operating, investing and financing. This will help further to compute the three categories of cash flows.

| Tran # | Cash/ Non-cash | Type | Cash flow | Comments |
|---|---|---|---|---|
| 1 | Non-cash | - | - | This is a credit sale |
| 2 | Cash | Operating | $12,000 | Cash is collected against accounts receivable |
| 3 | Non-cash | - | - | This is a credit buy |
| 4 | Non-cash | - | - | No cash is paid for the goods. The expense is only recognized now. |
| 5 | Cash | Operating | -$7,500 | Cash is paid against accounts payable |
| 6 | Cash | Investing | -$4,000 | This is a cash buy of PP and E |
| 7 | Cash | Investing | $1,500 | This is a cash sale of PP and E |
| 8 | Cash | Financing | -$500 | This is cash payment forloan |
| 9 | Cash | Financing | $1,000 | This is a cash receipt from new stock |
| 10 | Non-cash | - | - | Depreciation is not a cash expense |
| 11 | Cash | Operating | -$250 | This is a cash outflow for interest on loan |
| 12 | Non-cash | - | - | Accrual is not a cash expense |
| 13 | Cash | Operating | -$1,500 | This is cash paid for work |
| 14 | Non-cash | - | - | Only recording is not a cash expense |
| 15 | Cash | Operating | -$400 | This is cash paid for tax |

Once the above has been captured, the Statement of Cash Flows can be prepared as below. It may be noted that operating, investing and financing activities are recorded separately on the statement of cash flows.

**Statement of Cash Flows**
**For Year ended December 31, 2010**

| Cash flows from Operating Activities: | |
| --- | --- |
| Collection on account | $12,000 |
| Payment for inventory purchase | ($7,500) |
| Payment for misc expenses | ($1,500) |
| Payment of interest | ($250) |
| Payment of income tax | ($400) |
| Net cash provided by Operating Activities | $2,350 |
| **Cash flows from Investing Activities:** | |
| Purchase of PP and E | ($4,000) |
| Sale of PP and E | $1,500 |
| Net cash used by Investing Activities | ($2,500) |
| **Cash flows from Financing Activities:** | |
| Stock issue | $1,000 |
| Repayment of long-term debt | ($500) |
| Net cash provided by Financing Activities | $500 |
| Net increase in cash* | $350 |
| Beginning cash balance* | $250 |
| Ending cash balance* | $600 |

*In the above statement of cash flows, the last three lines summarize the cash positions. The "Net Increase in cash" is computed by adding the net cash values of operating, investing and financing activities. The "Beginning cash balance" is directly picked up from the Balance Sheet from last year. The "Ending cash balance" is computed by adding net increase in cash to beginning cash balance.

## Indirect Method

This method starts from the other financial statements, namely Balance Sheet and Income Statement. Using the data in these two, the Statement of Cash Flows is prepared. In order to do so we would need the Balance Sheet for the previous year as well to view changes in the various items.

This method is a little more complex but due to the use of computers, it is preferred by most companies as it does not need any additional information to create other than the availability of balance sheet and income statement. Readers of statement of cash flows prepared using this method might find it a little more difficult to read but the advantage of this method is it gives insights into where the money is going.

### Step 1 – Get Balance Sheet (two years), Income Statement (one year) and Notes to Financial Statements

The first requirement to prepare statement of cash flows using this method is the availability of balance sheet and income statement. Below are example balance sheet (for two years) and income statement (for one year only).

| Balance Sheet | 2010 | 2009 |
|---|---|---|
| **Current Assets:** | | |
| Cash | $1,630 | $500 |
| Accounts receivable | $1,800 | $2,300 |
| Inventory | $1,900 | $2,000 |
| **Long-term Assets:** | | |
| Property, plant, and equipment | $4,500 | $4,000 |
| Less accumulated depreciation | $1,000 | $1,300 |
| Property, plant, and equipment - net | $3,500 | $2,700 |
| Total Assets | $8,830 | $7,500 |
| **Current Liabilities:** | | |
| Accounts payable | $2,000 | $2,200 |
| Taxes payable | $100 | $80 |
| Interest payable | $20 | $0 |
| **Long-term Liabilities:** | | |
| Long-term debt | $2,500 | $3,000 |
| **Stockholders' equity:** | | |
| Common stock | $1,000 | $500 |
| Retained earnings | $3,210 | $1,720 |
| Total Liabilities and Equity | $8,830 | $7,500 |

**Income Statement For 2010**

| | |
|---|---|
| Sales | $15,000 |
| Gain on sale of equipment | $100 |
| **Expenses:** | |
| Cost of goods sold | $10,000 |
| Misc expenses | $2,760 |
| Depreciation expense | $460 |
| Interest expense | $100 |
| Total Expenses | $13,320 |
| Income before taxes | $1,780 |
| Income tax expense | $290 |
| Net Income | $1,490 |

The Note to the financial statement of 2010 mentions the following activities of buying and selling property, plant, and equipment

Sold PP and E worth $540 and bought PP and E worth $1,700

## Step 2 – Identification of increase and decrease in all current assets and liabilities

The following table shows increases and decreases in the current assets and liabilities from 2009 to 2010 by using the values from the balance sheet

| Item | Type | Nature of change | Change |
|------|------|------------------|--------|
| Cash | Current Asset | Increase | $1,130 |
| Accounts receivable | Current Asset | Decrease | $500 |
| Inventory | Current Asset | Decrease | $100 |
| Accounts payable | Current Liability | Decrease | $200 |
| Tax payable | Current Liability | Increase | $20 |
| Interest payable | Current Liability | Increase | $20 |

## Step 3 – Identify non-cash expenses, gains and losses

Under the indirect method operating cash flow starts with the Net Income for the year. We then add non-cash expenses to it as no cash has actually been spent on such expenses. In most cases it is only the depreciation expense. In some cases, amortization is also to be considered, if present in the balance sheet and expense statement. In our case only depreciation is present.

Gains and losses on long-term assets, like property, plant and equipment are also to be adjusted in the operating cash flows. Any gain is subtracted and loss is added. Hence, if a gain is made in selling a long-term asset, then the gain amount is to be deducted from the cash flows from operating activities. This is simply because such a gain will be later on considered in the cash flows from investing activities. If we don't adjust the amount here then it would lead to double counting in operating as well as investing cash flows. We have a gain on PP and Ementioned in the income statement.

## Step 4 – Preparing cash flow from operating activities

The idea of preparing this cash flow is to make adjustments to cash on the basis of how much cash has been consumed or recovered from current assets and liabilities. For example, if inventory increases, additional amount of cash gets blocked and, hence, that additional amount needs to be subtracted from the Net Income. Similarly, if the accounts payable increases, it means that the company has managed to get additional credit which has saved cash. Hence, this difference will be added to the Net Income. In this way all the increases and decreases in current assets and liabilities identified in the previous step are either subtracted or added to the Net Income to get cash flow from operating activities as below.

**Cash flows from Operating activities:**

| | | |
|---|---|---|
| Net Income | | $1,490 |
| Add depreciation expense | $460 | |
| Gain on sale of PP and E | ($100) | |
| Decrease in accounts receivable | $500 | |
| Decrease in inventory | $100 | |
| Decrease in accounts payable | ($200) | |
| Increase in tax payable | $20 | |
| Increase in interest payable | $20 | |
| | | $800 |
| Net cash provided by Operating activities | | $2,290 |

It may be noted that the above statement does not take into account the increase in Cash as a current asset. When the entire statement of cash flows is completed it will show this change. Cash is the only current asset that does not appear in the cash flows from operating activities. It is the outcome of the entire cash flow statement and hence it appears at the end.

## Step 5 – Preparing cash flow from investing activities

There is no change in any long-term assets other than PP and E. The Notes above mention these changes. Hence, it is straight forward to create cash flows from investing activities as below.

**Cash flows from Investing activities:**

| | | |
|---|---|---|
| Sold PP and E | $540 | |
| Purchased PP and E | ($1,700) | |
| Net cash used in Investing activities | | ($1,160) |

## Step 6 – Preparing cash flow from financing activities

All the information required for this is contained in the balance sheet for the two years. There is also one entry at the end of the income statement that, if present, will also be included in this cash flow. That entry is Dividend paid. It appears after the Net Income and strictly speaking is not a part of the income statement itself. In the current case no dividend has been paid. Below table shows the changes in the financing activities followed by their entries in the cash flows from financing activities.

| Item | Nature of change | Change |
|------|------------------|--------|
| Long-term debt | Decrease | $500 |
| Common stock | Increase | $500 |

Note above that Retained earnings does not figure as an item as it is not a financing activity but purely through the company's profits. Hence, it never shows up on the cash flow statement – it is not a cash flow at all.

**Cash flows from Financing activities:**

| | |
|---|---:|
| Repaid long-term debt | ($500) |
| Issued common stock | $500 |
| Net cash provided by financing activities | $0 |

## Step 7 – Consolidation of all three cash flows

The above three separate cash flows are consolidated into a single statement of cash flows as below

**Statement of Cash Flows For 2010**

**Cash flows from Operating activities:**

| | | |
|---|---:|---:|
| Net Income | | $1,490 |
| Add depreciation expense | $460 | |
| Gain on sale of PP and E | ($100) | |
| Decrease in accounts receivable | $500 | |
| Decrease in inventory | $100 | |
| Decrease in accounts payable | ($200) | |
| Increase in tax payable | $20 | |
| Increase in interest payable | $20 | |
| | | $800 |
| Net cash provided by Operating activities | | $2,290 |
| **Cash flows from Investing activities:** | | |
| Sold PP and E | $540 | |
| Purchased PP and E | ($1,700) | |
| Net cash used in Investing activities | | ($1,160) |
| **Cash flows from Financing activities:** | | |
| Repaid long-term debt | ($500) | |
| Issued common stock | $500 | |
| Net cash provided by financing activities | | $0 |
| Net increase in cash | | $1,130 |
| Beginning cash balance | | $500 |
| Ending cash balance | | $1,630 |

The final value of the ending cash balance should match with the value in 2010 balance sheet Cash. Beginning cash balance comes from Cash shown in the balance sheet from 2009.

## Solved Examples

**5.1 XYZ Inc. has the following transactions.**

a) Paid suppliers

b) Sold plant

c) Paid dividend

d) Purchased a 90-day treasury bill

e) Issued equity shares

Classify them under the following:

   i. Operating activity

  ii. Investing activity

 iii. Financing activity

 iv. Non-cash activity

   v. None of the above

**Solution:**

a) **Paid suppliers** – Operating activity

b) **Sold plant** – Investing activity

c) **Paid dividend** – Financing activity

d) **Purchased a 90-day treasury bill** – Operating activity

e) **Issued equity shares** –Financing activity

## 5.2 Balance sheet and income statements for ABC Inc. are given below. Prepare a Statement of Cash Flows.

| Balance Sheet | 2010 | 2009 |
|---|---|---|
| **Current Assets:** | | |
| Cash and bank balances | $25 | $20 |
| Current investments | $10 | $5 |
| Inventories | $160 | $138 |
| Accounts receivable | $120 | $115 |
| Loans and advances | $50 | $60 |
| **Long-term Assets:** | | |
| Long-term investments | $20 | $20 |
| Fixed assets | $550 | $495 |
| **Total Assets:** | **$935** | **$853** |
| | | |
| **Current Liabilities:** | | |
| Short-term provisions | $150 | $138 |
| **Long-term Liabilities:** | | |
| Secured loans | $180 | $160 |
| Unsecured loan | $100 | $100 |
| **Stockholders' equity:** | | |
| Paid-in capital | $125 | $125 |
| Retained earnings | $380 | $330 |
| **Total Liabilities and Equity** | **$935** | **$853** |

**Income Statement For 2010**

| | |
|---|---:|
| Sales | $1,065.00 |
| Cost of goods sold | $805.00 |
| Gross profit | $260.00 |
| Depreciation | $50.00 |
| Selling, general, and administrative expenses | $40.00 |
| Profit before interest and tax | $170.00 |
| Interest | $35.00 |
| Profit before tax | $135.00 |
| Tax | $50.00 |
| Net Income | $85.00 |
| Dividends | $35.00 |

## Solution:

One point to note here is that there are no Notes to financial statements given. Hence, we assume that only new PP and E has been bought as they have increased in value. Now, in order to find out how much new PP and E has been bought we need to find the difference between 2010 value of fixed assets and 2009 value of fixed assets. To this we should add the depreciation expense for 2010 as that would give us the gross fixed asset value. Below is the calculation.

New PP and E = $550 - $495 + $50 = $105

**Statement of Cash Flows For 2010**

**Cash flows from Operating activities:**

| | | |
|---|---:|---:|
| Net Income | | $85 |
| Add depreciation expense | $50 | |
| Increase in current investments | ($5) | |
| Increase in inventories | ($22) | |
| Increase in accounts receivable | ($5) | |
| Decrease in loans and advances | $10 | |
| Increase in short term provisions | $12 | |
| | | $40 |
| Net cash provided by Operating activities | | $125 |
| **Cash flows from Investing activities:** | | |
| Purchased PP and E | ($105) | |
| Net cash used in Investing activities | | ($105) |
| **Cash flows from Financing activities:** | | |
| Took secured loans | $20 | |
| Paid dividends | ($35) | |
| Net cash used by financing activities | | ($15) |
| Net increase in cash | | $5 |
| Beginning cash balance | | $20 |
| Ending cash balance | | $25 |

## Practice Exercise

5.1 XYZ Inc. has the following transactions.

a) Redeemed debentures

b) Received interest on debentures

c) Received dividend on equity investments

d) Obtained a computer on lease

e) Paid interest

f) Purchased an office

g) Exchanged land for equity in a subsidiary

Classify them under the following:

   i. Operating activity

  ii. Investing activity

 iii. Financing activity

 iv. Non-cash activity

   v. None of the above


5.2 During the year 2010, the following changes occurred in the current assets and liabilities of ABC Inc.

a) Prepaid insurance increased by $5,000

b) Accounts receivable reduced by $20,000

c) Inventory of raw materials increased by $2,000

d) Accounts payable decreased by $6,500

Depreciation for the year was $10,000 and the Net Income stood at $50,000. There were no gains or losses from any sale of PP and E. Use this data to create a statement of cash flows from operating activities.

5.3 Balance sheet and income statements for ZZZ Inc. are given below. It is further given that PP and E worth $500 was purchased during the year. Prepare a Statement of Cash Flows.

| Balance Sheet | 2010 | 2009 |
|---|---|---|
| Current Assets: | | |
| Cash and bank balances | $1,180 | $550 |
| Inventories | $450 | $500 |
| Accounts receivable | $400 | $200 |
| Long-term Assets: | | |
| Fixed assets | $2,200 | $1,850 |
| Total Assets: | $4,230 | $3,100 |
| | | |
| Current Liabilities: | | |
| Accounts payable | $400 | $300 |
| Short-term loans | $180 | $300 |
| Long-term Liabilities: | | |
| Long-term loan | $750 | $500 |
| Stockholders' equity: | | |
| Preferred stock | $200 | $100 |
| Paid-in capital | $600 | $400 |
| Retained earnings | $2,100 | $1,500 |
| Total Liabilities and Equity | $4,230 | $3,100 |

**Income Statement For 2010**

| | |
|---|---|
| Sales | $3,000.00 |
| Cost of goods sold | $1,500.00 |
| Gross profit | $1,500.00 |
| Depreciation | $150.00 |
| Selling, general, and administrative expenses | $100.00 |
| Profit before interest and tax | $1,250.00 |
| Interest | $75.00 |
| Profit before tax | $1,175.00 |
| Tax | $175.00 |
| Net Income | $1,000.00 |
| Dividends | $400.00 |

This page is intentionally left blank

# Glossary

**A**ccounting equation: Assets = Liabilities + Equity

**Accounts payable:** amount the company has to pay against its credit purchase

**Accounts receivable:** amount the company has to receive against a credit sale

**Accrued liabilities:** amount that the company has already incurred but not yet paid, like accrued wages, accrued interest etc.

**Accumulated depreciation:** total depreciation on an asset, like building or equipment, accumulated over the years

**Additional paid-in capital:** amount invested by stockholders over and above the paid-in capital or the par value

**Amortization:** process of allocating cost of intangible assets over a period of time

**Asset:** something that may give future benefits due to ownership or control based on a past transaction

**B**alance sheet: a financial statement that gives a snapshot of a company's resources (assets), obligations (liabilities), and owners' equity

**Bond:** an agreement between a seller and buyer where the seller agrees to repay the buyer an amount on maturity along with interest payments, either in instalments or at the end

**Bookkeeping:** preservation of a systematic, quantitative record of financial transactions

**C**ash: currency notes, coins and balance in bank accounts

**Cash dividends:** profit distribution to company's stockholders based on number of shares held

**Common stock**: a certificate representing ownership in a corporation. It gives voting rights and share in the profit of the company.

**Corporation:** a separate legal entity created by the state, owned by one or more persons, and having rights, privileges, and obligations that are distinct from those of its owners

**Cost of goods sold:** cost of manufacturing or buying an item that is sold in the normal course of business

**Credit:** a facility extended to a buyer to pay at a future date for a sale

**Current assets:** assets that are intended for use within one year

**Current liabilities:** obligations expected to be completed within one year

**Current portion of long-term debt:** that portion of long-term debt that is payable within one year

**epreciation:** process of allocating cost of assets over a period of time based on the time in which the company receives their benefits

**Direct method:** a way of preparing statement of cash flows directly from financial transactions

**Disclosure:** method of reporting non-quantitative information in financial statements

**Discontinued operations:** disposal of a part of the business

**Dividends:** a way of distribution of profits of the company with shareholders

**E**arnings per share (EPS): amount of net income associated with each share of the company

**Equity:** difference between assets and liabilities that reflects the money invested by the owners

**Expanded accounting equation:** Assets = Liabilities – Paid-in capital + (Revenues – Expenses) – Dividends

**Expenses:** amount consumed while transacting business by a company

**Extraordinary items:** gains and losses from transactions that are unusual and infrequent in nature

**F**inancial statements: summary information of a company's performance using balance sheet, income statement, statement of cash flows, notes etc.

**G**enerally Accepted Accounting Principles (GAAP):** set of accounting rules set by the local agency responsible for setting standards, like FASB

**Goodwill:** a competitive advantage enjoyed by a firm due to its intangible assets like, staff, rating, reputation etc.

**Gross profit:** difference between selling price and cost price of a product or service

**I**ncome from continuing operations:** income generated from those operations that are expected to continue in future

**Income statement:** reports the net income earned by the company over the defined period, generally a quarter or year

**Intangible assets:** non-physical assets like, goodwill, trademark etc.

**Inventory:** common term used to describe stored raw materials, in-process goods and finished products until they are sold

**Investment securities:** composed of publicly traded stocks and bonds

**L**ease:** a contract between two parties that temporarily gives the right over the property of one to the other over a specified period of time for a specified amount

**Long-term debt:** long-term loans, notes, debentures, mortgages etc.

**M**ortgage:** a loan secured by an asset pledged to the lender

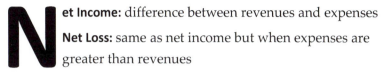

**N**et Income: difference between revenues and expenses

**Net Loss:** same as net income but when expenses are greater than revenues

**Notes to financial statements:** additional information provided in the financial statements

**O**perating income: measure of income that assesses the company's main business performance

**Owners' equity:** owners' share in the company

**P**aid-in capital: amount of money invested by the company's stockholders against shares of the company

**Par value:** face value of one share of the company – generally $1

**Preferred stock:** a class of stock that is similar to debt and provides a fixed stated return to preferred stockholders

**Prepaid expenses:** payment made in advance like, insurance paid for the entire year

**Property, plant, and equipment:** long-term assets like, land, building and machinery

**R**etained earnings: that portion of profits (or losses) that have been retained by the company instead of being paid as dividends to stockholders

**Revenue:** amount of money made by the company through its business activities, interest receipts etc.

**S**ales: a type of revenue made by the company in normal course of business

**Shareholders:** investors in a company

**Statement of cash flows:** a financial statement that gives all inflows and outflows of cash

**T**reasury stock: name given to stocks of a company when they are bought back by them

Made in the USA
Columbia, SC
11 August 2019